Ada
Lead

HAWKSMERE

Published by Hawksmere plc

12-18 Grosvenor Gardens

London SW1W 0DH.

A CIP catalogue record for this Pocketbook is available
from the British Library.

ISBN 1 85418 163 7

Printed in Great Britain by Ashford Colour Press.

Designed and typeset by Paul Wallis for Hawksmere.

Front cover: *Apollo Moon Landing*

Business Action Pocketbooks

Business Action Pocketbooks are concise but comprehensive reference books designed to fit in your pocket or briefcase to be a ready source of business information.

Pocketbooks will be of use to anyone involved in business. For owner managers and for managers in bigger businesses they will provide an introduction to the topic; for people already familiar with the topic they provide a ready reminder of key requirements.

Other titles in the 'Pocketbook' series

Building Your Business

This *Pocketbook* provides practical information about growth, strategy and business planning. Effective leadership, problem solving, decision making and the formal aspects of running a business are also covered in this guide which will help to define your strategy and ensure that you achieve your stake in the future.

Managing and Employing People

Discover the key to successful people management by motivating, stimulating and rewarding your staff. Practical information and advice about recruiting staff, employee rights and obligations, effectively managing people and the legal aspects of employment are all covered in this *Pocketbook*.

Finance and Profitability

Practical tips and techniques for profitable manage-ment, including costing and budgeting, record keeping and using financial statements and under-standing and finding investment are given in this *Pocketbook*. There is also advice on financial forecasting, monitoring performance against your plans and retaining effective financial control. This book will help ensure that your business is successful and profitable.

Sales and Marketing

This *Pocketbook* is an excellent reference tool focusing on the overall process of sales and marketing. It will help give you a direction and a set of goals along with practical tips and techniques for successful market research, segmentation and planning, promoting, selling and exporting. It will help you take those first important steps towards establishing a presence in your market.

Developing Yourself and Your Staff

Team building, personal development, managing meetings, stimulating staff and quality management are all covered in a clear and practical way for the busy manager in this *Pocketbook*. By developing your people through teamwork, training and empowerment you are developing your business – this book tells you how.

Effective Business Communications

Effective communications are vital to the success of your business. Every business needs to be able to communicate – to customers, staff, owners and other shareholders – in a number of ways – in writing, visually and in person. This *Pocketbook* provides an introduction to different forms of communication for a range of different purposes. The way a business communicates, and the information it provides, are of paramount importance to the business ability to survive and prosper.

Managing Projects and Operations

In any business, tasks may be continuous, such as production lines, or stand alone, discrete projects. All need to be carefully managed, with targets and milestones, if you are to maximise efficiency and effectiveness. This pocketbook provides an introduction to task management including decision making, corporate policies, planning and systems.

Public Relations Techniques that Work

In this pocketbook the author uses 30 years experience of both sides of the journalism/PR fence to provide valuable, practical advice on effective public relations. From the role of the PR officer to fees and costs and the effective use of PR in radio and television, this step-by-step guide details the 'rules' and steps to be taken in order to develop successful media relations. Helpful case studies add extra practitioner value to this excellent guide.

Contents

3 **The leader as decision-maker**

4 **Communication and presentation**

5 Personal reminders and thoughts worth thinking

1 Leadership and teambuilding

This chapter of the book is divided into two parts:

1. Leadership and
2. Teambuilding.

Part 1: Leadership

A survey of successful chief executives on the attributes most valuable at top levels of management indicated the following in order of rating:

1. Ability to take decisions
2. LEADERSHIP
3. Integrity
4. Enthusiasm
5. Imagination
6. Willingness to work hard
7. Analytical ability
8. Understanding of others
9. Ability to spot opportunities
10. Ability to meet unpleasant situations
11. Ability to adapt quickly to change
12. Willingness to take risks
13. Enterprise
14. Capacity to speak lucidly
15. Astuteness
16. Ability to administer efficiently

17. Open-mindedness

18. Ability to 'stick to it'

19. Willingness to work long hours

20. Ambition

21. Single-mindedness

22. Capacity for lucid writing

23. Curiosity

24. Skill with numbers

25. Capacity for abstract thought

There is (has and probably always will be) a debate about the differences and overlaps of leadership and management. Current opinion is that they are different concepts but they overlap considerably.

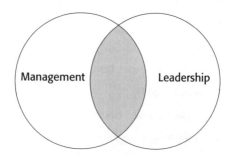

Perhaps management has the overtone of carrying out objectives laid down by someone else. It is certainly true that a well-managed business, in the sense of having perfect organisation, still needs that extra something.

Leadership has five distinctive nuances not found in management.

A leader must:

1. **Give direction**

2. **Provide inspiration**

3. **Build teams**

4. **Set an example**

5. **Be accepted.**

Henri Fayol (in 1916) divided the activities of an industrial company into six main groups:

1. **Technical** – production, manufacture and adaptation.

2. **Commercial** – buying, selling and exchange.

3. **Financial** – search for and optimum use of capital.

4. **Security** – protection of property and people.

5. **Accounting** – stocktaking, balance sheet, costs and statistics.

6. **Administration** – forecasting and planning, organising, commanding, co-ordinating and controlling.

Good administration is the hallmark of good management and the proper and efficient use of resources. Managers become leaders when their personality and character, their knowledge and functional skills of leadership are recognised and accepted by the others involved.

Leadership can be 'specific to the particular situation' and its 'authority' can derive from:

1. **position** (as in job title, rank or appointment),

2. **personality** (as in natural qualities of influence) and

3. **knowledge** (as in technical professional skills).

Fayol listed these following qualities as being needed by a person in 'command'. A person in command should:

- have a thorough knowledge of employees

- eliminate the incompetent

- be well versed in the agreements binding the business and its employees

- set a good example

- conduct periodic audits of the organisation and use summarised charts to further this review

- bring together the chief assistants by means of conferences at which unity of direction and focusing of effort are provided for

- not become engrossed in detail

- aim at making unity, energy, initiative and loyalty prevail among all employees.

The seven qualities of leadership

A leader is the kind of person (with leadership qualities) who has the appropriate knowledge and skill to lead a group to achieve its ends willingly. This section will look at the qualities and functions of leadership.

Personality and character cannot be left out of leadership. There are certain generic leadership traits, the seven important ones are:

1. Enthusiasm
Try naming a leader without it!

2. Integrity
Meaning both personal wholeness and sticking to values outside yourself, primarily goodness and truth – this quality makes people trust a leader.

3. Toughness
Demanding, with high standards, resilient, tenacious and with the aim of being respected (not necessarily popular).

4. Fairness
Impartial, rewarding/penalising performance without 'favourites', treating individuals differently but equally.

5. Warmth
the heart as well as the mind being engaged, loving what is being done and caring for people – cold fish do not make good leaders.

6. Humility
The opposite of arrogance, being a listener and without an overwhelming ego.

7. Confidence
Not over-confidence (which leads to arrogance), but with self-confidence which people know whether you have or have not got it.

In testing whether or not you have the basic qualities of leadership, you should ask yourself these questions.

	YES	NO
Do I possess the above mentioned seven qualities? (This 'test' will subsequently reveal whether or not you really do!)	☐	☐
Have I demonstrated that I am a responsible person?	☐	☐
Do I like the responsibility and the rewards of leadership?	☐	☐
Am I well-known for my enthusiasm at work?	☐	☐
Have I ever been described as having integrity?	☐	☐
Can I show that people think of me as a warm person?	☐	☐
Am I an active and socially participative person?	☐	☐
Do I have the self-confidence to take criticism, indifference and/or unpopularity from others?	☐	☐

	YES	NO
Can I control my emotions and moods or do I let them control me?		
Have I been dishonest or less than straight with people who work for me over the past six months?		
Am I very introvert, very extrovert (or am I an ambivert – mixture of both – as leaders should be)?		

If leadership depends on the situation, you need to ask yourself, whatever your qualities, whether you are right for the situation:

	YES	NO
Are your interests, aptitudes and temperament suited to your current field of work?		
If not, can you identify one that would better suit you where you would emerge as a leader?		
Do you have the 'authority of knowledge' in your current field (and have you acquired all the necessary professional and specialist skills through training that you could have done at this point in your career?)		
Are you experienced in more than one field/industry/function?		
Are you interested in fields adjacent and relevant to your own?		
Do you read situations well and are you flexible in your approach to changes within your field?		

Functions of leadership

In leadership, there are always three elements or variables:

1.   The leader
Qualities of personality and character.

2.   The situation
Partly constant, partly varying.

3.   The group
The followers: their needs and values.

This section of the book looks at leadership functions in relation to the needs of work groups. These needs can be seen as three overlapping needs:

1.   Task need
To achieve the common task.

2.   Team maintenance needs
To be held together or to maintain themselves as a team.

3.   Individual needs
The needs which individuals bring with them into the group.

These three needs (the task, team and individual) are the watchwords of leadership and people expect their leaders to:

- help them achieve the common task
- build the synergy of teamwork and
- respond to individuals and meet their needs.

The **task** needs work groups or organisations to come into being because the task needs doing and cannot be done by one person alone. The task has needs because pressure is built up to accomplish it to avoid frustration in the people involved if they are prevented from completing it.

The **team maintenance** needs are present because the creation, promotion and retention of group/organisational cohesiveness is essential on the 'united we stand, divided we fall' principle.

The **individual** needs are the physical ones (salary) and the psychological ones of:

- recognition
- a sense of doing something worthwhile
- status
- the deeper need to give and to receive from other people in a working situation.

The Task, Team and Individual needs overlap:

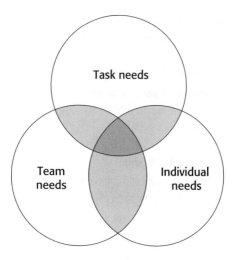

This overlapping is evident in that:

- achieving the task – builds the team and satisfies the individuals

- if team maintenance fails (the team lacks cohesiveness) performance on the task is impaired and individual satisfaction is reduced

- if individual needs are not met – the team will lack cohesiveness and performance of the task will be impaired.

Leadership exists at different levels:

Team leadership
Of teams of about 5 to 20 people.

Operational leadership
A significant must in a business or organisation comprising a number of teams whose leaders report to you.

Strategic leadership
A whole business or organisation, with overall accountability for the levels of leadership below you.

At whatever level of leadership, Task, Team and Individual needs must be constantly thought about. To achieve the common task, maintain teamwork and satisfy the individuals, certain functions have to be performed. A function is what leaders do as opposed to a quality which is an aspect of what they *are*.

These functions (the functional approach to leadership, also called action-centred leadership) are:

- Defining the task
- Planning
- Briefing
- Controlling
- Evaluating
- Motivating
- Organising
- Providing an example

Leadership functions in relation to Task, Team and Individual can be represented by this diagram:

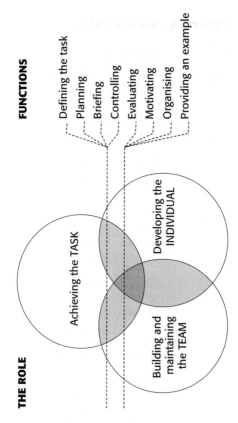

Leadership functions

These leadership functions need to be handled with excellence and this is achieved by performing those functions with increasing skill.

Before examining the skills of leadership, it is worth seeing where certain **qualities** of leadership can

be viewed as having functional value. These can
be examined as leadership characteristics.

Leadership characteristics

The need	*Quality*	*Functional value*
Task	Initiative	gets the group moving
	Perseverance	prevents the group giving up
	Efficiency	work done well knowing costs (energy, time and money)
	Honesty	establishing facts
	Self-confidence	facing facts
	Industry	steady application pays dividends
	Audacity	when not to be restrained by rules or convention
	Humility	facing up to mistakes and not blaming others

The need	Quality	Functional value
Team	Integrity	integrating the team and creating trust
	Humour	relieving tension and maintaining a sense of proportion
	Audacity	inspire through originality or verve
	Self-confidence	trusted by others
	Justice	fair dealing builds group discipline
	Honesty	wins respect
	Humility	not selfish, shares praise, not arrogant and divisive
Individual	Tact	sensitive in dealing with people
	Compassion	sympathetic awareness and help
	Consistency	people know where they stand
	Humility	recognises qualities/abilities and gives credit
	Honesty	wins individual respect
	Justice	fair-dealing encourages individuals

Leaders need to exhibit the following attributes/
qualities/characteristics in exercising the functions:

1. *Group influence*
To generate a group willingness to achieve a desired
goal/objective.

2. *Command*
To decide upon a course of action as quickly as the
situation demands and to carry it through with a
firmness and strength of purpose.

3. *Coolness*
To remain cool or unperturbed under testing or
trying conditions.

4. *Judgement*
Ability to arrange available resources and information
in a systematic and common sense way to
produce effective results.

5. *Application/responsibility*
To demonstrate sustained effort combined with a
degree of dependability in order to complete a task
or achieve an objective.

Leadership skills

Having identified the main functions or principles of leadership, there are skills in providing those functions in different situations and managers need to develop their abilities to bring those skills to bear in increasing levels of excellence.

The eight functions (defining the task, planning, briefing, controlling, evaluating, motivating, organising and setting an example) will now be examined.

1. Defining the task

A task is something that needs to be done. People in organisations and teams need to have this distilled into an objective which is:

- clear

- concrete

- time-limited

- realistic

- challenging

- capable of evaluation.

There are five tests to apply to the defining of a task and they are:

i) Do you have a clear idea of the objectives of your group now and for the next few years/ months which have been agreed with your boss?

ii) Do you understand the overall aims and purpose of the organisation?

iii) Can you set your group's objectives into the context of those larger intentions?

iv) Is your present main objective specific, defined in terms of time and as concrete/tangible as you can make it?

v) Will the team know for itself if it succeeds or fails and does it get speedy feedback of results?

In defining the task/communicating the objective you need to have the following abilities:

- To tell the group the objective you have been given

  BEWARE: *not understanding it yourself can lead to lack of clarity.*

- To tell the group what to do and why

  BEWARE: *giving the reason in terms of a past event rather than future.*

- To break down aims into objectives for other groups

  BEWARE: *not making them specific enough or not making sure there are enough objectives which add up to complete the aim.*

- To agree the objective

  BEWARE: *taking things for granted and not fixing on the objective.*

- To relate the aim to the purpose (to answer what and why questions)

  BEWARE: *confusing your division's aim with the purpose of the organisation.*

- To define the purpose and check that the aims relate to it and to each other

  BEWARE: *not doing it often enough.*

- To redefine the purpose to generalise it and create more aims and objectives

  BEWARE: *causing confusion by doing it too often or not knowing that it has to be done.*

- To communicate purpose to employees

  BEWARE: *using the wrong language, by-passing leaders below you or relying on others doing it for you.*

In defining the task, it needs to be broken down into objectives, aims and purpose so that it can be communicated with clarity. The end of the task should also be defined when the need arises and all should be aware of what the success criteria will be.

2. Planning

This key activity for any team or organisation requires a search for alternatives and that is best done with others in an open-minded, encouraging and creative way. Foreseeable contingencies should always be planned for.

Planning requires that the what, why, when, how, where and who questions are answered. Plans should be tested…

Checklist to test plans

	YES	NO
Have I called upon specialist advice?	☐	☐
Have all feasible courses of action been considered and weighed up in terms of resources needed/available and outcomes?	☐	☐
Has a programme been established which will achieve the objective?	☐	☐
Is there a provision for contingencies?	☐	☐
Were more creative solutions searched for as a basis for the plan?	☐	☐
Is the plan simple and as foolproof as possible, rather than complicated?	☐	☐
Does the plan include necessary preparation or training of the team and its members?	☐	☐

In ensuring that there is the appropriate level of participation in the planning process, the chart below may be useful:

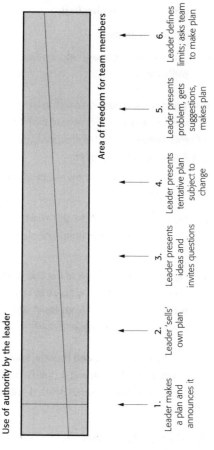

The planning continuum

3. Briefing

Briefing or instructing a team is a basic leadership function conducted usually in a face-to-face way. Any briefing is an opportunity to:

- create the right **atmosphere**

- promote **teamwork**

- get to know, encourage and motivate each **individual**.

Before and after any briefing session, to ensure that the question of 'what is my role in all this?' (which will be on everyone's mind) is answered, you need to ask yourself these questions:

1. Does every individual know exactly what his/her job is?

2. Does each member of the team have clearly defined targets and performance standards agreed with me?

3. Does each person know at the end what is expected of him/her and how that contribution or that of his/her team fits in with the purposeful work of everyone else?

Communicating (speaking **and** listening) is crucial to get right in any briefing and it centres on the task, team and individual needs which should be addressed.

The effective speaking attributes of a successful briefing are to be:

- prepared

- clear

- simple
- vivid
- natural.

Assertiveness can be important. For example, to give the task direction and in explaining the role of the team/individual, especially in an initial briefing or where there is low morale.

In briefings, you could do worse than keep these points in mind:

The Adair short-course on leadership

1. The six most important words…
   'I admit I made a mistake'.

2. The five most important words…
   'I am proud of you'.

3. The four most important words …
   'What is your opinion?'

4. The three most important words…
   'If you please'.

5. The two most important words…
   'Thank you'.

6. The one most important word…
   'We'.

7. The last, most *unimportant* word…
   'I'.

4. *Controlling*

Excellent leaders get maximum results with the minimum of resources.

To control others, leaders need to exhibit self-control (but remembering that anger/sadness can be legitimate responses if the circumstances warrant it and are themselves mechanisms for control), to have good control systems (simple and effective to monitor financial and task performance) and to have control of what it is that others should and should not be doing in order to meet objectives. The success at directing, regulating, restraining or encouraging individual and team efforts on the task (and in meetings) are the criteria for testing a leader's effectiveness as a 'controller'.

A checklist for testing controlling skills

	YES	NO

Do I maintain a balance
between controlling too tightly
or giving too much freedom to
the team?

Am I able to co-ordinate work-
in-progress, bringing together
all the parts in proper relation
with each other?

In technical work, do I ensure
that team and individual needs
are met?

Do meetings I chair run over
time(s) allotted to topics?

Do I have proper budgets and
ways of monitoring actual
performance?

Do customers rate my organisation's control systems for:

- quality of product/service

- delivery

- costs

- safety?

5. Evaluating

Leaders need to be good at:

- assessing the consequences
- evaluating team performance
- appraising and training individuals
- judging people.

In *assessing the consequences*, leaders should be able to foresee the outcome of action (or inaction) in terms of the technical, the financial and the human and to ask probing questions of the team in order to establish the likely consequences.

In *evaluating team performance*, perhaps through a de-briefing session after a particular project, the performance of the team as a whole in relation to the task can be examined:

- Has it been a success, a partial success or a failure?
- Can lessons be learnt?
- Can action be taken to improve performance?
- What feedback can be given to **ensure** improvement?

The evaluation of the team is helpful in trying to build it into a high-performance one where the hallmarks are:

- clear realistic objectives
- shared sense of purpose
- best use of resources
- atmosphere of openness

- handles failure
- rides out the storms.

In *appraising and training individuals*, the following agenda can be used:

- Past performance
- Future work to be done: targets, priorities, standards and strategies
- Matching perceptions of what can be expected by each party of the other in order to achieve a good working relationship
- Improving skill, knowledge, behaviour.

Some tips in handling appraisals:

- Have all necessary data available
- Put the other person at ease
- Control pace and direction of the interview
- Listen… listen… listen
- Avoid destructive criticism (encourage self-criticism)
- Review performance systematically
- Discuss future action
- Discuss potential/aspirations
- Identify training/development required
- Avoid common pitfalls, such as:
  - dominating the conversation
  - making promises unlikely to be kept
  - expecting dramatic changes overnight
  - blaming those not present.

In *judging people*, leaders decide who should do what and this always affects outcomes and so is a crucial skill. Leaders should not have favourites because:

- it destroys team unity

- the favourite is a personification of your judgement about people – if others do not agree with your judgement, your credibility suffers

- favourites advance by recognising the social and esteem needs of their bosses and by pandering to them – the boss can have his/her judgement impaired by this.

Judgement is improved by analysing impressions formed, discussing them with others and by making decisions about people more slowly and after deliberation.

In evaluation, you need to ensure that:

- your decision-making judgement is good

- you appraise people regularly and well

- you are good at judging people

- you evaluate your own performance as much as those who work for you.

6. *Motivating*

There are six key principles for motivating others:

1. Be motivated yourself

2. Select people who are highly motivated

3. Set realistic and challenging targets

4. Remember that progress motivates

5. Provide fair rewards

6. Give recognition.

Individuals are motivated by their requirements to satisfy a (Maslow's) hierarchy of needs:

- Physiological – hunger, thirst, sleep
- Safety – security, protection from danger
- Social – belonging, acceptance, social life, friendship and love
- Esteem – self-respect, achievement, status, recognition
- Self-actualisation – growth, accomplishment, personal development.

Each individual will be at a different stage/level up this hierarchy of needs and will need to be motivated accordingly.

Other than in financial terms, individuals are usually motivated if they can see that they will be given:

- achievement
- recognition
- job interest
- responsibility
- advancement.

A good leader provides the right climate and the opportunities for these needs to be met on an individual basis and this is perhaps the most difficult of a leader's challenges.

Leaders must also inspire others. In 1987, James Kouzes and Barry Posner identified five characteristics of what they call exemplary leaders:

1. Leaders challenge the process. Leaders search for opportunities. They experiment and take risks, constantly challenging other people to exceed their own limitations.

2. Leaders inspire a shared vision. Leaders envision an enabling future and enlist people to join in that new direction.

3. Leaders enable others to act. Leaders strengthen others and foster collaboration.

4. Leaders model the way. Leaders set the example for people by their own leadership behaviour and they plan small wins to get the process moving.

5. Leaders encourage the heart. Leaders regard and recognise individual contributions and they celebrate team successes.

7. Organising

Good leaders are good at:

*   organising themselves – their own work and particularly how they manage themselves, their time and how they delegate

*   organising the team – to build and maintain it to ensure that there is good, effective team-work

*   organising the organisation – the structure and the systems/processes in which, and by which, people operate.

Leaders change things and organise for the achievement of results – leading change requires considerable powers and skills of leadership. In all aspects, leaders must organise with a purpose clearly in mind at all times.

Leaders should consider their organising skills by reference to the Task, Team and Individual as follows:

*   **Task: Is there a common purpose?**
    *   is the task broken down into aims and objectives?
    *   how is it/are they communicated?

*   **Team: what are the teams/sub-teams?**
    *   how do they contribute to the purpose?
    *   do they relate together as a team?

*   **Individual: do they have freedom and discretion?**
    *   are individual needs being met?

Further questions in surveying your organisation are:

- Do the Task/Team/Individual circles overlap sufficiently to provide and maintain high morale in the face of difficulties?

- How are tensions resolved and are there adequate systems/disciplinary procedures/ dispute handling methods in place?

The size of working teams/groups should be examined to assess the importance of these factors:

- Task/technology – complexity narrows the span of control, ie. is the team too big to control/handle this aspect and does it mesh properly with other teams?

- Communications – especially with geographical/physical dispersement, are they good enough?

- Motivation and autonomy – is the training commensurate with any wishes to be self-sufficient?

- Competence of leaders – are large teams led by good enough leaders, what are the leader's other commitments and does he/she have good/specialist support?

A checklist to test the organising function ability

	YES	NO

You

Can you organise your personal and business life in ways which would improve your effectiveness as a leader? ☐ ☐

Do you delegate sufficiently? ☐ ☐

Can you identify improvements in your time management? ☐ ☐

Team

Is the size and make-up correct? ☐ ☐

Should a sub-team be set up? ☐ ☐

Are opportunities/procedures in place to ensure participation in decision-making? ☐ ☐

Do you restructure and change individual's jobs as appropriate? ☐ ☐

*A checklist to test the organising
function ability (continued)*

	YES	NO

Organisation

Do you have a clear idea of its
purpose and how the parts
should work together to
achieve it?

Are effective systems in place
for training/recruitment/
dismissal?

Do you carry out surveys into
the size of teams, number of
leadership levels, growth of
unnecessary complexity, line
and staff co-operation and
properly working communications systems?

Are you good at administration,
recognising the performance of
administrators and ensuring
that administrative systems
facilitate excellent performance
from teams/individuals?

8. Setting an example

'Leadership is example'. To be successful, a good leader must 'walk the talk'. Employees take a fraction of the time to know a leader as he/she takes to get to know them. The example you are giving is quite simply you. Whether this is a good or a bad example depends on the leader.

An example is set in verbal and non-verbal ways and all aspects of a leader's words and deeds must be considered in the light of this.

If example is contagious, it is worth ensuring that a good one is set to encourage the qualities sought in others.

Some key questions for good leadership are:

- Task – do you lead from the front/by example?

- Team – do you develop your teams' standards through the power of example?

- Individual – do you view each individual as a leader in their own right?

Bad example, particularly of hypocrisy, is noticed more than good, so care must be taken in all that a leader says and does.

A checklist to test if you set a good example

	YES	NO
Do you ask others to do what you would be unwilling to do yourself?	☐	☐
Do people comment on the good example you set in your work?	☐	☐
Does your (bad) example conflict with what all are trying to do?	☐	☐
Can you quote when you last deliberately set out to give a lead by example?	☐	☐
Can you think of ways you could lead by example?	☐	☐
Do you mention the importance of example to team leaders who report to you?	☐	☐

Developing leadership skills

Organisations (and if you are the leader of one that means you) should ensure that they have a policy of developing the leadership potential in all and particularly of newly appointed 'leaders'! Individuals should also ensure that they focus on developing their leadership skills by training, reading, analysing and following the example of good leaders and by assessing, monitoring and improving their own performance.

Part 2: Teambuilding

This section looks at teambuilding from the leadership perspective and, as has been seen, teambuilding is part of the leadership 'holy' trinity of Task, Team and Individual.

One of the main results of good leadership is a good team:

Good leadership characteristics	Team outcomes
Enthusing	Team members are purposefully busy and have a basis to judge priorities
Lives values such as integrity	Gives a sense of excitement and achievement with people willing to take risks and higher work loads
Leads by example	Consistency in knowing leader's values
Generates good leaders from followers	Is trusted

Good leadership characteristics	Team outcomes
Aware of own behaviour and environment	Aspire to leader's example
Intellect to meet job needs	Confidence in leadership
Aware of team and individual needs	The led start to lead (with leader less indispensable) being delegated to, coached and supported
Exhibits trust	Inspires confidence and performance
Represents the organisation to the team and vice versa	Confidence of contribution to aims and commitment to them

In 1985, ICI believed that the outcomes of effective leadership were that people will:

- have a clear sense of direction and work hard and effectively
- have confidence in their ability to achieve specific challenging objectives
- believe in and be identified with the organisation
- hold together when the going is rough
- have respect for and trust in managers
- adapt to the changing world.

In achieving the task, building the team and developing the individual, whilst leadership style may differ, effective leadership (in ICI's findings and its development courses) emphasized that the leader must do the following:

- feel personally responsible for his/her human, financial and material resources
- be active in setting direction and accepting the risks of leadership
- be able to articulate direction and objectives clearly and keep his/her people in the picture
- use the appropriate behaviour and methods to gain commitment for the achievement of specific objectives
- maintain high standards of personal performance and demand high standards of performance from others.

Leaders in teambuilding provide the functions of:

- planning
- initiating
- controlling
- supporting
- informing
- evaluating.

In relation to teambuilding and the leader's role in terms of the Task, Team and Individual (which need to be addressed if the Team is to perform at high levels of achievement) the following three sets of questions will help analyse and improve the way that teams operate.

1. Task

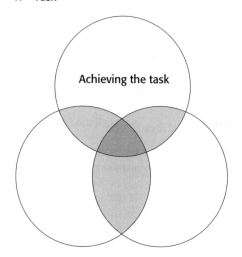

Purpose:	Am I clear what the task is?
Responsibilities:	Am I clear what mine are?
Objectives:	Have I agreed these with my superior, the person accountable for the group?
Programme:	Have I worked one out to reach objectives?
Working conditions:	Are these right for the job?
Resources:	Are these adequate (authority, money, materials)?
Targets:	Has each member clearly defined and agreed them?
Authority:	Is the line of authority clear (Accountability chart)?
Training:	Are there any gaps in the specialist skills or abilities of individuals in the group required for the task?
Priorities:	Have I planned the time?
Progress:	Do I check this regularly and evaluate?
Supervision:	In case of my absence who covers for me?
Example:	Do I set standards by my behaviour?

2. Team

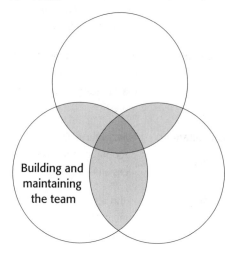

Building and maintaining the team

Objectives: Does the team clearly understand and accept them?

Standards: Do they know what standards of performance are expected?

Safety standards: Do they know consequences of infringement?

Size of team: Is the size correct?

Team members: Are the right people working together? Is there a need for sub-groups to be constituted?

Team spirit: Do I look for opportunities for building teamwork into jobs? Do methods of pay and bonus help to develop team spirit?

Discipline:	Are the rules seen to be reasonable? Am I fair and impartial in enforcing them?
Grievances:	Are grievances dealt with promptly? Do I take action on matters likely to disrupt the group?
Consultation:	Is this genuine? Do I effectively encourage and welcome ideas and suggestions?
Briefing:	Is this regular? Does it cover current plans, progress and future developments?
Represent:	Am I prepared to represent the feelings of the group when required?
Support:	Do I visit people at their work when the team is apart? Do I then represent to the individual the whole team in my manner and encouragement?

3. Individual

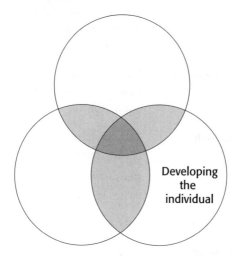

Targets: Have they been agreed and quantified?

Induction: Does she/he really know the other team members and the organisation?

Achievement: Does she/he know how his/her work contributes to the overall result?

Responsibilities: Has she/he got a clear and accurate job description? Can I delegate more to him/her?

Authority: Does she/he have sufficient authority for his/her task?

Training: Has adequate provision been made for training or retraining both technical and as a team member?

Recognition: Do I emphasise people's successes? In failure is criticism constructive?

Growth: Does she/he see the chance of development?

Does she/he see some pattern of career?

Performance: Is this regularly reviewed?

Reward: Are work, capacity and pay in balance?

The task: Is she/he in the right job? Has s/he the necessary resources?

The person: Do I know this person well? What makes him/her different from others?

Time/attention: Do I spend enough with individuals listening, developing, counselling?

Grievances: Are these dealt with promptly?

Security: Does she/he know about pensions, redundancy and so on?

Appraisal: Is the overall performance of each individual regularly reviewed in a face-to-face discussion?

The good leader in teambuilding must act as:

- encourager

- harmoniser

- compromiser

- expediter/gatekeeper

- standard setter

- group observer/commentator

- follower.

As leader, there must be a clear understanding of:

i) Team properties

- common background/history (or lack of it)

- participation patterns

- communication

- cohesiveness

- atmosphere

- standards

- structure

- organisation

- changes over time (forming, storming, norming and performing) both progressive and regressive

- how to change the team properties in evidence.

ii) *Team roles being defined, but with room left for individual personality*

iii) *Team member functions*

- distinction between content (the what) and process (the how) of group functioning

- difference between behaviour related to the task and behaviour related to maintenance of the team and that behaviour which expresses individual idiosyncrasies

- team leader functions (as above).

iv) *The individual*

- balancing interests and self-expression of individuals and the team

- the value of the task draws individuals/team together

- having sound values motivates individuals in teams.

v) *The overlapping needs of Task, Team and Individual need to be addressed*

vi) *Team processes*

- to see what is really going on

- improved decision-making rests on seeing beneath the surface the pressures that influence the team

- calmness creates interdependence within the team and with the leader

- avoid team flight into abstractions

- aim for consensus (only where possible)

- assess team view of authority to see how processes/decisions are being affected by it.

vii) Teams within teams

- watch out for hostility, communication failure and mistrust as signs of team fragmentation

- develop teamwork between teams as well as within them

- winning can be as destructive to teams as losing, if not worse, unless both outcomes are handled well

- be aware of teams within teams and act accordingly to regain cohesiveness or sub-divide.

Summary and six-month follow up test

Summary

Leadership centres on:

- the leader – qualities of personality and character
- the situation – partly constant, partly varying
- the team – the followers: their needs and values
- the overlapping needs of the Task, Team and Individual
- leadership functions can be summarised as:
    - defining the task
    - planning
    - briefing
    - controlling
    - evaluating
    - motivating
    - organising
    - providing an example

Teambuilding centres on:

- achieving the task
- building and maintaining the team
- developing the individual.

Six-month follow-up test

Do individuals have personal development plans?

Are people working well as individuals and in teams?

Have you analysed your leadership strengths/weaknesses and addressed your own development needs?

Have you noticed that morale and motivation is up in yourself and others?

Are things getting done?

Do you constantly focus on Task, Team, Individual?

2 Motivation and people management

Introduction

Getting the best from people, achieving results through individuals and teams, maintaining consistent high performance, inspiring oneself and others into action – all depend on the skills of motivation. Self-motivation can be as difficult as motivating others and you cannot have one without the other.

Adair's eight rules in motivating people

1. Be motivated yourself

2. Select people who are highly motivated

3. Treat each person as an individual

4. Set realistic and challenging targets

5. Remember that progress motivates

6. Create a motivating environment

7. Provide fair rewards

8. Give recognition

Understanding what moves an individual to action is crucial in a manager being able to engage the will to act. Motives (which operate the will which leads to action) are inner needs or desires and these can be conscious, semi-conscious or unconscious. Motives can be mixed, with several clustered around a primary motive.

The 50:50 rule

Just as the Pareto principle (or 80:20 rule) is the ratio of 'the vital few and trivial many', the Adair 50:50 rule has it that:

> **50 per cent of motivation comes from within a person; and**
>
> **50 per cent from his or her environment, especially from the leadership encountered therein.**

Unfortunately human behaviour and what decides/triggers it is more complicated than the carrot and stick 'theory' which deals only with external stimuli. The 'carrot' of reward/incentive and the 'stick' of fear of consequences reveal only two 'motives' which govern action. There are many more!

The expectancy theory – formulated by Edward C Tolman in the 1930s – (whereby behaviour rests on the instinctive tendency for individuals to balance the value of expected benefits against the expenditure of energy) falls into the same 'stimulus-response' approach to motivation. It does demonstrate, however, that an individual's strength of motivation can be affected by the expectations of outcomes from certain actions and further strengthened by the individuals preferred outcome, as demonstrated by Victor H. Vroom in the 1960s.

It pays, therefore, in external stimuli to bear in mind that:

1. **the routes to desired outcomes for individuals and teams are clear; and**

2. **individuals perceive the rewards or punishments in different ways according to their own values.**

This confirms the need to treat people as individuals but as the 50:50 rule also indicates, other motivational factors should always be set in the context of the individual's managed environment. Other theories of motivation which suggest that 90% of motivation is within an individual should be tempered by the 50:50 rule.

Needs and motivation

Maslow's hierarchy of needs

A sketch map of individual needs – which is useful for managers when considering individuals – can be drawn from Maslow's hierarchy of needs (1954), but it must be borne in mind that his theory does not fully appreciate individual differences or that each person has a unique set of needs and values.

Maslow identified five motivating factors in his hierarchy of needs and indicated that as each need is satisfied, others then emerge. He identified:

1. **physiological needs (including hunger, thirst, sleep)**

2. **safety needs (security and protection from danger)**

3. **social needs (belonging, acceptance, social life, friendship and love)**

4. **self-esteem (self-respect, achievement, status, recognition)**

5. **self-actualisation (growth, accomplishment, personal development).**

However, points to bear in mind are that:

- individuals do not necessarily move up the hierarchy on the principle that a 'satisfied need ceases to motivate' although that can be the case

- different levels of needs can kick in at random points on the scale toward full satisfaction of needs

- culture and age and other factors can affect the importance of the different needs to different people and at different stages in their lives

- the satisfying of some needs can be sacrificed in order to try and satisfy higher level needs.

McGregor's Theory X and Theory Y

In 1960 in his book 'The Human Side of Enterprise', McGregor demonstrated that the way in which managers manage depends on the assumptions made about human behaviour. He grouped these assumptions into Theory X and Theory Y.

Theory X – the traditional view of direction and control

i) The average human being has an inherent dislike of work and will avoid it if possible.

ii) Because of this dislike of work, most people must be coerced, controlled, directed, threatened with punishment to get them to give adequate effort toward the achievement of organisational objectives; and

iii) The average human being prefers to be directed, wishes to avoid responsibility, has relatively little ambition and wants security above all.

Theory Y – the integration of individual and organisational goals

i) The expenditure of physical and mental effort in work is as natural as play or rest;

ii) External control and the threat of punishment are not the only means for bringing about effort toward organisational objectives. People will exercise self-direction and self-control in the service of objectives to which they are committed;

iii) Commitment to objectives is a function of the rewards associated with their achievement;

iv) The average human being learns, under proper conditions, not only to accept, but to seek responsibility;

v) The capacity to exercise a relatively high degree of imagination, ingenuity and creativity in the solution of organisational problems is widely, not narrowly, distributed in the population.

vi) Under the conditions of modern industrial life, the intellectual potentialities of the average human being are only partially utilized.

McGregor drew on Maslow for much of Theory Y and put forward the cluster of features as an unproven hypothesis and further research was needed (Herzberg) to seek to prove it correct.

In terms of management in practice Theory Y does reveal that in any individual within an organisation there are untapped resources of goodwill, energy, creativity and intelligence.

Herzberg's Motivation – hygiene theory

In Herzberg's research (published in his 1959 book 'The Motivation to Work'), fourteen factors were identified to be the sources of good or bad feelings:

1. **Recognition**

2. **Achievement**

3. **Possibility of growth**

4. **Advancement**

5. **Salary**

6. **Interpersonal relations**

7. **Supervision – technical**

8. **Responsibility**

9. **Company policy and administration**

10. **Working conditions**

11. **Work itself**

12. **Factors in personal life**

13. **Status**

14. **Job security**

The eight '**hygiene**' factors, according to Herzberg, which can create job dissatisfaction are:

1. Company policy and administration

- availability of clearly defined policies, especially those relating to people

- adequacy of organisation and management

2. Supervision – technical

- accessibility, competence and fairness of your superior

3. Interpersonal relations

- relations with supervisors, subordinates and colleagues

- quality of social life at work

4. Salary

- total compensation package, such as wages, salary, pension, company car and other financially related benefits

5. Status

- a person's position or rank in relation to others, symbolised by title, size of office or other tangible elements

6. Job security

- freedom from insecurity, such as loss of position or loss of employment altogether

7. Personal life

- the effect of a person's work on family life, eg stress, unsocial hours or moving house

8. Working conditions

- the physical conditions in which you work

- the amount of work

- facilities available

- environmental aspects eg ventilation, light, space, tools, noise

The six **motivating** factors that lead to job satisfaction were identified by Herzberg as being:

1. Achievement

- specific successes, such as the successful completion of a job, solutions to problems, vindication and seeing the results of your work

2. Recognition

- any act of recognition, whether notice or praise (separating recognition and reward from recognition with no reward)

3. Possibility of growth

- changes in job where professional growth potential is increased

4. Advancement

- changes which enhance position or status at work

5. Responsibility

- being given real responsibility, matched with necessary authority to discharge it

6. The work itself

- the actual doing of the job or phases of it.

The **hygiene** factors are those where people seek to avoid particular situations, whereas the **motivating** factors are matched with people's needs to achieve self-actualisation or self-realisation.

Satisfaction of the Herzberg motivators and avoidance of problems with the hygiene factors can help you as a manager to assess roles and jobs within your organisations to check what job-enrichment or empowerment you ought to contemplate to improve performance and give individuals greater job satisfaction.

Managers/leaders and motivation

Managers and leaders should take a realistic and visionary view of people who work for them and with them. Individuals can be managed better if it is recognised that they are:

1. individuals, but become fully developed and truly themselves in relation to other people and meaningful work

2. creative and imaginative, but only in concert with others through working on their own or in teams

3. driven by achievement (as individuals) but know that they achieve more as part of a team

4. self-motivated and self-directed but need management/leadership (if only to co-ordinate activities)

5. intelligent enough to know the difference between rewards such as money and those less tangible rewards that meet value needs

6.   interested in leaving work/the world a better place and know that that yields a bonus

As has been described in the relevant section earlier in the book, in leadership, the achievement of the task, the building and maintaining of the team and the development of the individual can only result from motivating people by providing the leadership functions of:

- planning

- initiating

- controlling

- supporting

- informing

- evaluating

and by being able to inspire others.

Managers should check that individuals have:

1.   a sense of achievement in their job and feel that they are making a worthwhile contribution to the objective of the team

2.   jobs which are challenging and demanding with responsibilities to match capabilities

3.   adequate recognition for achievements

4.   control over delegated duties

5.   a feeling that they are developing along with growing experience and ability.

Manager's motivating checklist

Do you   YES NO

Agree with subordinates their
main targets and responsibilities together with standards of
performance, so that you can
both recognise achievement?   ☐   ☐

Recognise the contribution of
each member of the team and
encourage team members to
do the same?   ☐   ☐

Acknowledge success and
build on it?   ☐   ☐

Analyse set-backs, identifying
what went well and giving
constructive guidance to
improve future performance?   ☐   ☐

Delegate as much as possible
giving more discretion over
decisions and accountability to
a sub-group or individual?   ☐   ☐

Show those that work with you
that you trust them or do you
surround them with unneces-
sary controls?   ☐   ☐

Do you   **YES**   **NO**

Provide adequate opportunities
for training and re-training if
necessary?

Encourage each individual to
develop his/her capacities to
the full?

Review the overall performance of each individual
regularly face-to-face?

Match financial reward to
contribution?

Make time to talk and listen so
that you understand the
unique and changing profile of
needs and wants in each
person and work with what you
find?

Encourage able people with
the prospect of promotion
within the organisation?

Getting the best from people

Be motivated yourself

Enthusiasm and motivation inspires others and the badges of good example setting are that you should be:

- public – make sure you act in the open

- spontaneous – do not appear calculated

- expressive – do things because they are natural to you not for effect

- self-effacing – setting a good example is not glory-seeking.

Motivation is contagious so you should be infectious! If you are not motivated yourself, you cannot motivate others and you should examine the reasons why you lack motivation. Symptoms include having little or no interest in the job, wanting to arrive late and leave early, wanting to leave the job, feeling active dislike for it and feeling out of place in it.

You can strengthen your motivation by reminding yourself:

1. to feel and act enthusiastically and in a committed way in your work

2. to take responsibility when things go wrong rather than blaming others

3. to identify ways you can lead by example

4. act on the 50:50 principle

5. to motivate by word and example rather than manipulation

6. set an example naturally rather than in a calculated way

7. not to give up easily

8. to ensure you are in the right job for your own abilities, interests and temperament

9. to be able to cite experiences where what you have said or done has had an inspirational effect on individuals, the team or the organisation

10. that the three badges of leadership are enthusiasm, commitment and perseverance.

Select people who are highly motivated

The seven key indicators of high motivation are:

1. energy – not necessarily extrovert but alertness and quiet resolve

2. commitment – to the common purpose

3. staying power – in the face of problems/difficulties/set-backs

4. skill – possession of skills indicates aims and ambitions

5. single-mindedness – energy applied in a single direction

6. enjoyment – this goes hand in hand with motivation

7. responsibility – willingness to seek and accept it.

Choosing people well (and mistakes are made which should be confronted and remedied early) means looking at motivation, ability and personality and you should, when interviewing, look for real evidence behind the interviewee's facade.

Looking for the Michelangelo motive (where the quality of the work itself is a key motivator) can yield good results in selecting highly motivated individuals. You should look for:

- a sense of pride in the individual's own work
- an attention to detail
- a willingness to 'walk the extra mile' to get things right
- a total lack of the 'its good enough, let it go' mentality
- an inner direction or responsibility for the work (without the need for supervision)
- an ability to assess and evaluate own work, independently from the opinions of others.

It should be stressed that perfectionism is not what is called for – the best can be the enemy of the good.

Managers should check whether individuals are in the right job with the right skills and abilities, otherwise motivation techniques will fail. The aim is to select people who are motivated for the most appropriate job.

Treat each person as an individual

Find out what motivates an individual, do not rely on generalised theories or assumptions. Enter into a dialogue with each team member – help them to clarify what it is that motivates them – and use what you find to mutual benefit.

In each person you should engender a sense of:

- trust
- autonomy
- initiative
- industry
- integrity
- security.

Take time with each individual to:

- encourage
- hearten
- inspire
- support
- embolden
- stimulate.

Ask yourself these questions to ensure that you treat each person as an individual:

1. **Do you know the names of people on your team and their teams if they are leaders?**

2. **Can you identify ways in which those who report to you differ from each other?**

3. **Do you accept that an individual's motivation changes from time to time?**

4. **Do you spend time with people to know them, work with them, coach them?**

5. **Does your organisation see you as an individual?**

Set realistic and challenging targets

This can only be done in the context of understanding the organisation's aims or purpose. It is only then that targets and objectives can be identified and tasks defined.

HOW?

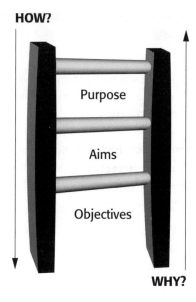

Purpose

Aims

Objectives

WHY?

Jacob's ladder model

Moving down the ladder, ask how are we going to achieve the task? The answer is by breaking down the purpose into the main aims and the main aims into short and long-term objectives or goals.

Moving up the ladder, ask why are we doing this? The answer is to achieve this objective in order to achieve this aim and to satisfy this purpose.

Targets (for short and longer-term objectives) set should be:

- specific
- clear
- time-bounded.

An objective or target must be realistic (feasible) and challenging. If you aim for the best you can often get it.

Targets must be agreed and monitored with further action agreed to maintain motivation toward shared objectives.

Remember that progress motivates

There is a 'lust to finish' (John Wesley) and the key principle is that progress motivates – moving forward leads them to raise their game.

Feedback on progress (or the relative lack of it) helps motivation either to spur people on or to concentrate the mind on what yet needs to be done.

Feedback is not given at all or sometimes not often enough, usually for these reasons:

- 'People don't need to be told how they are doing, they already know'

- 'People take it easy if you say things are going well'

- 'They are unhappy and cause trouble if you say things are not going well'

- 'We lack the skills or the time to do it'.

Feedback which is affirmative (praise) must be:

- accurate

- sincere

- generous

- spontaneous

- fair.

It must not be:

- patronising

- superior/condescending

- grudging

- calculated for effect.

Maintaining motivation depends on informing and inspiring and the rule is always to give information first, before you attempt to encourage.

Maintaining high morale is key to high motivation and morale covers the individuals and the team. Where an individual has low morale, the issues have to be addressed on an individual basis, but where group or team morale is low, the answer lies in deciding whether there is a lack of confidence:

- of ultimate success

- in the present plan(s)

- in the leadership/management

- in the minds of team members.

It can be necessary to remotivate the team by rebuilding self-confidence and by readdressing:

- aims – and clarifying objectives

- plans, resources needed

- leadership

- overlooked factors

- re-establishing the worth or value of the task(s)

- involvement of individuals in key decisions.

Create a motivating environment

Guidelines here are:

1. Beware of creating a restrictive organisation with an over-emphasis on controls

2. Avoid public criticisms of individuals

3. Ensure Herzberg's hygiene factors are catered for – the physical and psychological well-being of people should have high priority

4. Control systems should only be introduced where necessary

5. Give people an input into decisions which affect their working lives (especially in respect of substantial change)

6. Keep units and sub-units as small as possible (for large units tend to be bureaucratic and demotivational if they lack inspired leaders)

7. Pay attention to job design – avoid repetitive work, introduce variety

8. Give people autonomy and a job with a 'product' that an individual can recognise as his/her own

9. Ensure an individual understands the significance of their job in relation to the whole, which will also encourage new ideas and innovation.

Provide fair rewards

Although it is difficult to ensure that the financial reward an individual receives is fair (commensurate with contribution), effort must be applied in trying to get it right. There are other motivating 'returns' that individuals look for from jobs (as in Maslow's hierarchy of needs), but money is the one which has the main strategic importance for most people.

Most individuals like the combination of a fixed salary with a variable element related to performance or profits.

Also of tactical importance are incentives to improve performance in key areas eg sales, customer service and credit control.

Incentives can be in the form of cash, vouchers, merchandise or travel, but care must be taken to administer any incentive schemes fairly and without risking demotivating any 'losers'.

In providing fair rewards, an organisation should ask itself:

1. **Do we have a scheme whereby financial reward is made up of a fixed and variable element?**

2. **Do we link performance and pay?**

3. **Have we addressed the problems of whether to pay performance-related elements to the team or the individual?**

4. **Do we actively consider changing our information systems to improve methods of rewarding performance?**

5. **Do we have schemes other than for sales people?**

6. **Does our organisation reward the behaviours/performance that publicly it values?**

7. **Do senior managers have pay rises/bonuses when they expect others to do without them?**

It is always worth remembering Herzberg's insight that salary has more power to make people dissatisfied or unhappy than it has the power to motivate them.

Give recognition

Financial reward is seen by the recipient as a tangible form of recognition. There are other ways whereby appreciation is expressed for what has been contributed.

If recognition is not given, an individual can feel unnoticed, unvalued and unrewarded. This leads to a drop in motivation and energy levels.

Recognition should be formal or informal, for the individual and/or the team, as appropriate.

In giving recognition, you should try to ensure that you:

1. treat everyone in a fair and equal way

2. reward real achievements or contributions

3. reflect the core values of the organisation

4. use it to guide and encourage all concerned

5. give it in public if possible

6. give it formally and informally

7. give it genuinely and sincerely.

Other than financial payments, any words of recognition could be reinforced by giving:

- time off (with pay)

- tickets for an event or dinner out

- small gift

- special project of importance

- a change in job title.

It is a good idea to back up words of praise or recognition with some tangible gift.

Find out what is going on, share praise received with subordinates, and say thank-you more often, because people really value positive recognition and are motivated by it.

Know people's names – that is the basic form of recognition!

Summary and six-month follow-up test

To draw the best out of people you need to:

- be motivated yourself
- select people who are already motivated
- set challenging but realistic targets
- remember that progress motivates
- treat each person as an individual
- provide fair rewards
- give recognition.

Six month follow-up test

Are you motivated?

Are targets set and monitored with feedback being clearly given?

Do you consciously try to motivate people by understanding their needs and aspirations?

Do you spend time with individuals and teams working on motivating them?

Do you feel you are getting the best from people?

3 The leader as decision-maker

Management can be said to be 'deciding what to do and getting it done'.

Success in business stems from good quality management decisions first of all and then the effectiveness in implementation which depends on the skills of leadership, influencing, communication and motivation.

One survey (of 200 leaders of industry and commerce) ranked 'the ability to take decisions' as the most important attribute of top management.

The logical or rational leader will invariably follow this decision-making model:

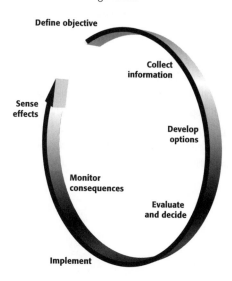

Define objective

Collect information

Sense effects

Develop options

Monitor consequences

Evaluate and decide

Implement

However, US research into decisions by public sector officials suggests that decision-makers rarely settle for the 'best' or optimum solution, being affected by emotion, power politics, the influences of other people and by their own values. Often a decision is a compromise between different courses of action, being one that:

- agrees to some extent with one's own personal interests, needs or values

- meets the value standards of superiors

- is acceptable to those affected (by the decision and for carrying it out)

- looks reasonable

- has an escape element of self-justification if it all goes wrong.

Clearly such approaches to decision-making must be removed from your approach!

Finally, leaders need to be prepared to make time to think about decisions – to devote quality time to this crucial area of activity; to avoid superficiality (resulting from performing a great variety of tasks with little time to spare) because thought must be as important as action; and to involve other people (colleagues, subordinates and superiors) in making sensible management decisions.

Key elements of effective thinking and decision-making

Analysis

An essential ability in analysing is to be able to break the whole up into its component parts, particularly complex matters into its simple elements.

The hallmarks of the analytical mind are that it:

1   establishes the relationship between the parts and the whole

2   finds the root cause(s) of the problem

3   identifies the issue(s) at stake, the 'either/or' upon which a decision rests.

Analytical ability is improved by:

*   working from first principles

*   establishing the facts and separating them from opinions, assumptions or suppositions

*   asking yourself questions (as in 'When did the problem first arise?' as well as our six friends Who, What, Why, When, Where and How?

*   constantly checking the premise and/or logical steps which can undermine good reasoning

*   thinking backwards from the desired outcome

*   organising the facts

*   seeing the problem as a solution in disguise.

Analysis is not, however, an end in itself and trying to over-analyse can lead to inactivity or 'paralysis by analysis' as it has been called.

Synthesis

Decision-making requires an individual to 'take a view' and that depends on the ability to combine parts or elements to form a whole: synthesis. Holistic is a useful word to use in this regard as it also conveys the approach, especially in business, which recognises that 'wholes' are produced by grouping various units together where it is difficult to analyse them into their parts without losing this wholeness. Hence an holistic view needs to be taken in business decision-making.

One difficulty is that analysis can be the enemy of synthesis (holism) and vice versa. There is a need in business to be able to see the wood for the trees (holism) rather than only the trees (analysis).

In this sense, and in business too, the whole is greater than the sum of its parts. Business thinking is a good example of the Gestalt approach whereby we arrive at an understanding of:

- the overall significance rather than a mechanistic explanation

- the relationships between events not just the events themselves which do not occur in isolation, only in a setting which gives each significance.

Managers need to take this whole view – not to see things as a marketing problem, or a production issue, or a stock control difficulty, or a people problem, or a management failure. Look at the whole to see what that can yield by way of a solutions.

Integration of facts, ideas and opinions is like the ability to synthesise and strengthens the manager's decision-making. Particularly in assessing financial performance, a manager needs to view the figures as a whole as well as in detail.

Other useful approaches

Imagination

This is an important attribute to have in business: the skill to visualise the whole in one's imagination. It is part and parcel of being creative in the approach to decision-making. Being imaginative is a crucial ability to develop in oneself and others: it helps to surprise the competition, to exploit the unexpected, to invent new products or services, or to solve problems creatively. Indicators of a healthy level of imagination are the abilities to:

*   recall events easily and visually

*   foresee what may happen before an event

*   be inventive or creative artistically, mechanically or verbally

*   fantasise about future events.

These elements of recall, visualising, creating, foreseeing and fantasising contribute to effective thinking in business as much as in the arts or scientific fields.

Conceptual thinking

Although a **concept** may appear to be an abstraction arrived at by analysis, it has a different feel because:

1 **it is a whole (and as such more than the sum of its parts); and**

2 **it is a developing entity in its own right.**

A concept is 'something conceived in the mind' and conceptual thinking in business addresses such issues as:

- What business are we in?

- What are its strengths/weaknesses?

- What are its purposes/aims?

Conceptual thinking should be kept separate from decision-making, even though decisions are made on the basis of the concepts that we have.

Concepts can be used in 'profiling' business development, but they then have to be made more specific in the form of proposals or plans, before being implemented. Concepts can be a way of taking your mind away from the particular and include the ideas of what ought to be as opposed to what is. Good quality concepts will underpin good quality business decisions. Therefore you should generate clear well-defined concepts and develop them.

Intuition

Being intuitive, successfully so, is undoubtedly a help in making effective decisions. It is not always possible to analyse problems into solutions and intuition is the useful power to know what has happened or what to do. Interestingly the powers of intuition are diminished by stress and general fatigue and so your ability to be insightful in decision-making can be adversely affected by these factors.

'Intuition', 'instinct', 'first impressions', 'feel', 'hunch' and 'flair' are important dimensions to explore when faced with not only decision-making, but also considering business activities and the systems to run them.

It is too easy to be dismissive of intuition, of being able to 'sense' what needs to be done or to 'smell' trouble/opportunities. Rather it is an invaluable key to making and taking effective decisions.

Originality and innovation

Creative and innovative thinking can help in making decisions that develop a business so they are elements to encourage in yourself and others. Be prepared to work at problems/issues to encourage creativity or insight coming into play and be prepared to encourage new ideas (by rewarding those who put them forward), to try out and innovate new products/services as well as new ways of doing things.

The concept of value in decision-making

With analysis and synthesis, valuing is the third essential in effective thinking and decision-making. The ability to make decisions has two main aspects:

1   To establish the truth or true facts; and

2   To know what to do.

Time must be taken on the first, otherwise integrity, or the value of truth, is lost in the process. Thinking first and then deciding what to do is the correct order in decision making. Getting at the truth should make knowing what to do easier.

In many respects, it is better to behave as if truth is an object, that it must be discovered. The truth and valuing what one discovers, should be seen as 'objective' with one's own views and conditioning recognised and relied on or discounted as needs be.

When you rely on others, as managers so often do, you may have to sift information from their 'valuations' (information plus judgement). This is another form of valuing – of knowing who and when to trust to give you truth, or truth backed by acceptable value judgements. Questioning is a valid part of establishing the credentials of the adviser and the credibility of the advice. Can you trust the person to tell the truth backed by sufficient expertise or insight? You will learn by experience to recognise the people who:

•   tell you what they think you want to hear

- express a view thinking it might agree with your own

- are watching their backs

- try to hide things.

Be scrupulous in establishing the truth – ask questions until you are satisfied you have it right.

You are good at valuing if you can say that invariably you have good judgement and the converse is also true. Knowing the truth or reality can then be followed by deciding what to do.

Also, beware of inaccurate figures (even from accounts departments!), errors in facts, figures and assumptions and specious assurances – all must be tested for accuracy and 'truth'.

Decision-making and weighing up the options

It is invariably necessary to choose a particular course of action out of a range of possible 'options'. What is the best way of ensuring that your own selection process is a sound one? The basic point here is that you should never assume that there is only one option open to you. Consider a number of options (or as many sensible and pertinent ones as you can muster), many of which will be directly dictated or affected by the facts that you can establish. Gathering information also helps the collection of options, even considering options that you might think are closed to you (eg increasing price, scrapping low-profit items etc).

Selecting and working through a range of options means considering:

- Which are the possible ones?

- Which of those are feasible?

- How to reduce feasible options to two choices, the 'either/or'?

- Which one to choose (or a mixture)?

- Whether any action is really necessary at all, now, later?

- Whether or not to keep options open, ie not to choose yet?

You should avoid any compulsion to take action through an option where no action would be better and you should avoid assuming that there are only two possibilities, until you have weighed up all the feasible ones you can in a reasonable time-frame.

Whilst considering the options beware false assumptions: test all for validity.

At the same time, it is essential to understand the other factors which can limit the range and choice of options or their applicability. Judgement (again beware false assumptions – including about these factors) is needed about:

1 **Time**

2 **Information**

3 **Resources**

4 **Knowledge.**

You have to know the real (not assumed) limits which the above factors can impose on the options available to you.

Generating options, particularly if, initially, there seems to be only one, will usually lead to better decision-making. This is where imagination, creative-thinking and intuition can help.

Considering fresh possibilities and suspending judgement whilst generating them (through brain-storming) can increase the range of options by avoiding negativity as in:

- 'It won't work'
- 'We do it this way'
- 'It can't be done'
- 'It failed before'.

In weighing the options you must refine your skills at considering the consequences, both the possible and the probable. This will lead to assessment of risk and reward and both should be carefully calcu-lated.

Can you accept the risk of failure – what is the worst that can happen if it fails and can I accept it?

Judgement then is used in selecting from the range of options which have been carefully weighed and assessed as to their probable outcomes.

It can be useful to clarify options or, in decision-making to seek to test by argument or discussion. If done in the right way clarity can be the result.

Disagreement should be encouraged, not for its own sake of course, but to stimulate ideas. Discussion prior to action should not be feared, but arguing badly (for example: being personal, over pernickety, seeking to procrastinate unnecessarily etc.) should be avoided.

Summary and six-month follow-up test

Six-month follow up test

DO YOU USE

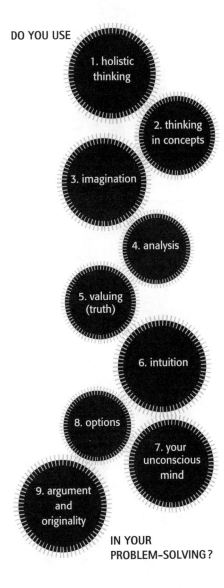

1. holistic thinking

2. thinking in concepts

3. imagination

4. analysis

5. valuing (truth)

6. intuition

8. options

7. your unconscious mind

9. argument and originality

IN YOUR PROBLEM-SOLVING?

4 Communication and presentation

Introduction

It is self evident that written and spoken communication skills are of crucial importance in business (and personal) life. Managers and leaders in particular must be effective communicators, good at getting their message across to, and at drawing the best out of, people. Communication skills in all forms, including non-verbal communication, need to be worked at and improved to ensure you understand people and they understand you.

Issues in communication

- You must be in social contact with the other person or people

- You must want to communicate

- It is better to risk familiarity than be condemned to remoteness

- The best way to empower others is to impart information (along with the delegated authority to make decisions and act on the information given)

- Get out of your office – meet, listen, provide information and give people the context in which they operate – to communicate and encourage

- Good communication is the core of customer care

- Remember customers (and suppliers) communicate with others about you

- To communicate with your customers you must handle complaints (as an organisation) as personally as possible – by a meeting or phone call in preference to letter or fax; you must listen to what customers suggest and communicate product/service changes/developments with them in advance

- Presentation skills are important in communicating with colleagues as well as customers/clients

- Meetings, internal and external are key indicators of a person's communication (including listening) skills

- Communication is a business requirement: establish proper systems and ensure all use them

- Remember the equation: size + geographical distance = communication problems

- Communicate with poor performers to improve their contribution and in appraisals be truthful, helpful and tactful

- Help others to improve their communication skills

- Assess your own communication skills and strive to improve them bit by bit. (Also, assess the communication skills of colleagues and identify areas for improvement).

Personal communication skills checklist

	YES	NO
Do you understand the importance of communication in your personal and business life?	☐	☐
Are you a good communicator? (Check with your partner at home, with friends and with colleagues).	☐	☐
Can you write down your strengths and weaknesses as a communicator? And have you listed them?	☐	☐

Have you identified a need to improve your communication skills in any or all of these areas and will you now set about doing so (reading further books and/or attending training seminars as needs be):

- listening
- reading
- writing
- one-to-one interviews
- speaking and presentation
- managing meetings
- within your organisation?

Are you motivated strongly to become an excellent communicator?	☐	☐

Listening

Listening has been called the forgotten skill in communication. It is more than just hearing, it is the giving of thoughtful attention to another person whilst they are speaking.

The 'disease of not listening' – the 'I hear what you say' response – exhibits the following symptoms:

- Selective listening is habit forming: not wanting to know things and turning a deaf ear to certain types of information does two things:

  i)   you do not listen to important items

  ii) people censor what they tell you

       and both can be damaging in business and in private life

- The constant interrupter is not listening (but planning his/her own next interruption)

- The 'day-dreamer' is not a listener

- The poor listener is easily distracted by external factors eg noise, heat/cold

- The lazy listener makes no effort with difficult information

- The poor listener over-reacts to a speaker's delivery and/or quality of visual aids rather than concentrating on what is being said.

The tell-tale signs of a good listener

- paying close attention to others when they are talking

- taking an interest in someone you meet for the first time, trying to find an area of mutual interest

- believing everyone has something of value to teach or impart to you

- setting aside a person's personality/voice in order to concentrate on what they know

- being curious in people, ideas and things

- encouraging a speaker (with nods or eye contact)

- taking notes

- knowing one's own prejudices and working at controlling them to ensure listening continues

- being patient with poor communicators

- not being told you don't listen

- having an open mind in respect of other peoples' points of view

Listening skills pivot on the five following attributes:

1. **Being willing to listen**

2. **Clearly hearing the message**

3. **Interpreting the meaning (the speaker's meaning, not only your interpretation)**

4. **Evaluating carefully (suspending judgement at first but then assessing value and usefulness)**

5. **Responding appropriately – remembering communication is a two-way street.**

In active listening you must be prepared to:

- ask questions

- weigh the evidence

- watch your assumptions

- listen between the lines (at what is not said and for non-verbal elements such as facial expressions, tone, posture, physical gestures etc.)

Reading skills

Good reading is listening in action – giving time and thought and remaining alert to the possibilities suggested. A good reader will try to work past:

- poor structure and layout

- boring style

- off-putting tone

- too much or too little information

- difficult to follow content

- inordinate length

- lack of illustrations/diagrams.

You should examine what materials you **must** read, **should** read or **might** read in the light of your job/role/future ambitions and then decide accordingly how and when to handle a particular item.

Speed reading is useful but only if it is accompanied by speed understanding and reading too fast (or too slowly) can impair understanding.

Read selectively (according to the must, should or might categorisation) from each item that confronts you. In this, scanning can help decide what attention to give particular items, so you should look at overall content (headings and sub-headings), sample the style and content of a few paragraphs, scan (if still interested) selected parts and then read that which you decide you are interested in. In reading carefully, you should be aware of the need to:

- be clear about your purpose of reading any piece of writing

- have questions in mind

- keep the questions firmly in mind and seek answers to them

- read for main ideas

- test the evidence, explanations and conclusions critically

- make notes as you progress

- test the writer's experience against your own

- consider whether or not to re-read

- discuss the material with others if appropriate

- reflect on what has been read.

Writing skills

Communicating in writing is an essential part of your job. There are three key elements in communicating on paper:

- Structure and lay-out

- Content

- Style and tone.

Writing should be thought of as talking to a person on paper and the six principles of good spoken communication apply – and they are:

1. **Clarity**

2. **Planning and preparation**

3. **Simplicity**

4. **Vividness**

5. **Naturalness**

6. **Conciseness.**

In letters, reports and memos the quality improves if the appropriate amount of planning is given to the points you wish to make and their order of importance. Further drafts can improve on the initial effort.

In writing a business letter you should always test the draft to ensure that:

1. the message is clear

2. points are made in the best order

3. it has the right style and tone

4. the most appropriate words and phrases are being used

5. the grammar/spelling is correct

6. the layout is attractive.

In writing reports which work the following points should be borne in mind:

- If the report is to stand alone and not to support a briefing or presentation it will need to be more than an aide-memoir

- A report should:
    - have an introduction with background and objectives
    - a title which indicates its purpose
    - be structured like a book with chapters, headings and sub-headings all clearly numbered and signposted
    - ensure the main body of evidence is succinct and in an easy to follow order
    - end with conclusions and suitable recommendations
    - indicate assumptions made
    - put complicated data into an appendix
    - use illustrations/diagrams to clarify points made

- Easy reading makes hard writing
- Churchill's guidelines for report writing centred on:
  - setting out main points in a series of short, crisp paragraphs
  - complicated factors or statistics should form an appendix
  - considering submitting headings only, to be expanded orally
  - avoiding woolly phrases, opting for conversational phrases
  - setting out points concisely aids clearer thinking
- Reports can be tested for their effectiveness as follows:
  - is the structure and layout clear and easy to follow?
  - is the content complete and does it:
  - state the purpose?
  - say when, by whom, for whom and with what scope it was prepared?
  - identify and address the problem clearly
  - ensure detail does not cloud the main issue
  - give sources for facts
  - use consistent symbols and abbreviations
  - use accurate figures
  - make clear statements

- have conclusions which flow logically from facts and their interpretation
- ensure other possible solutions are only abandoned with stated reasons?
- in general
- is the report objective?
- are criticisms of its recommendations pre-empted?
- is it efficient and business-like?
- does it offend anyone?
- can it be understood by a non-technical person?
- is it positive and constructive?
- does it point up the decision to be made and by whom?

The style and tone of written communications is important to ensure the message is put over, and received, clearly. Some rules are:

- keep it simple
- strive for clarity above all things (even above brevity)
- be natural
- be concise
- let the tone reflect your true feelings but beware being terse, curt, sarcastic, peevish, angry, suspicious, insulting, accusing, patronising or presumptuous
- be courteous (cordial and tactful).

Speaking and presentation skills

Effective speaking

There are certain principles to be followed to increase the power of communicating or expressing thoughts in spoken words.

Adair's six principles of effective speaking

1. **Be clear**
2. **Be prepared**
3. **Be simple**
4. **Be vivid**
5. **Be natural**
6. **Be concise**

Preparation is helped by asking the Who? What? How? When? Where? Why? of the speaking occasion to focus on the audience, the place, the time, the reasons giving rise to the occasion, the information that needs to be covered and how best to put it across.

Presentation skills

There are six clusters which form the main elements of good, effective presentation skills.

1. Profile the occasion, audience and location

You should ask yourself these questions:

- The occasion
    - what kind is it?
    - what are the aims of it?
    - what time is allowed?
    - what else is happening?
- The audience
    - do they know anything about you?
    - do you know its size?
    - what do they expect?
    - why are they there?
    - what is their knowledge level?
    - do you know any of the audience personally or professionally?
    - do you expect friendliness, indifference or hostility?
    - will they be able to use what they hear?
- The location
    - do you know the room size, seating arrangements, lay-out/set-up and acoustics?
    - do you know the technical arrangements for use of microphones, audio-visuals,

lighting and whether assistance is available (and have you notified in advance your requirements)?

- do you know who will control room temperature, lighting and moving people in and out

- have you seen it/should you see it?

2. Plan and write the presentation

Elements to address are:

- Deciding your objective which needs to be:

  - clear

  - specific

  - measurable

  - achievable in the time available

  - realistic

  - challenging

  - worthwhile

  - participative

- Making a plan with a framework which has:

  - a beginning (including introductory remarks, statement of objectives and relevance and an outline of the presentation(s))

  - a middle (divided into up to six sections maximum, ensuring main points are illustrated and supported by examples or evidence, use summaries and consider time allocation carefully – and test it)

  - an end (summarise, linking conclusions with objectives and end on a high note)

3. Use visual aids

As up to 50 per cent of information is taken in visually, careful consideration should be given to the clear, simple and vivid use of audio-visuals.

Useful tips are:

- Overhead/projector slides help make a point and keep eye contact with an audience (look at the people not the slides)

- Only present essential information in this way (keep content to about 25 words or equivalent if in figures)

- Prepare them with appropriate professionalism

- Know the order

- Use pictures and colour if possible

- Do not leave a visual aid on for too long

Some difficulties with the different types of audio-visual equipment are:

- Overhead projection: ease of use and flexibility can be offset by poor quality images and problems in using well

- 35mm slide projection: professional in appearance, good for large audience and easy to use with a remote control can be offset by the need for dim lights (making note-taking difficult) and lack of flexibility in changing order of viewing

- Flipcharts: are easy to use and informal but difficult to use successfully with large groups and generally do not look professional and take up time to use

- Computers/tape decks/videos: can provide variety but difficult to set-up and synchronise, especially without technical support

4. Prepare your talk

In preparing your talk you need to decide whether you are to present with a full script, notes or from memory. This depends on the occasion and purpose of the presentation but whichever method is chosen, it is always acceptable to refer to your fuller notes if needs be during a presentation. Notes on cards or on slides/flipcharts can be used as memory joggers if you present without notes. If you are required to read a paper, at least be able to look up occasionally. Remember that failing to prepare is preparing to fail.

5. Rehearse with others

Rehearsal is important, but not so much that spontaneity is killed and naturalness suffers, to ensure the presentation (and any audio-visual aid) is actually going to work in practice.

You should always visit the location if at all possible and check that everything works – knowing the location is as important as rehearsing the presentation, indeed it is an essential part of the rehearsal.

6. Delivery on the day

Overall you should ensure that your presentation's:

- **beginning** – introduces yourself properly, captures the audience and gives the background, objectives and outline of your talk.

- **middle** – is kept moving along (indicating whether questions are to be asked as-you-go or at the end) with eye contact over the whole audience, at a reasonable pace, with a varying voice and obvious enjoyment on your part.

- **end** – is signalled clearly and then goes off with a memorised flourish.

- **questions** – are audible to all (or repeated if not), answered with conciseness, stimulated by yourself asking some questions, dealt with courteously and with the lights on.

- **conclusion** – is a strong summary of talk and questions/ discussions and closes with words of thanks.

If you find you are nervous (and this is normal) experiencing fear and its physical manifestations, remember to:

1. Breathe deeply

2. Manage your hands

3. Look at your audience

4. Move well

5. Talk slowly

6. Compose and relax yourself

7. Remember that the audience is invariably on your side

8. Project forward to the end of the presentation and picture the audience applauding at the end.

One-to-one interviews

Such meetings have the common characteristics that they are (usually) pre-arranged, require preparation and have a definite purpose.

Unless it happens to be a dismissal, one-to-one interviews require that:

- both parties know the purpose of the meeting (notified in advance)

- information to be exchanged should be considered in advance and answers at the meeting should be honest

- as interviewer you should keep control: stick to the point at the issue and the time allocated and give the other party adequate time to talk (prompting by questions if necessary).

The structure of the interview should be as follows:

- the opening – setting the scene, the purpose and a relaxed atmosphere

- the middle – stay with the purpose, listen, cover the agenda

- the close – summary, agree action, end naturally not abruptly on a positive note.

Sometimes it is useful to ask the right questions to obtain the required information/exchange. Questions to use are the open-ended, prompting, probing, or what-if questions, whilst the ones to avoid (unless being used for specific reasons) are the yes/no, closed, leading or loaded questions.

In performance appraisal interviews the aim should be to give constructive criticism in the following way:

1. In private

2. Without preamble

3. Simply and accurately

4. Only of actions that can be changed

5. Without comparison with others

6. With no reference to other people's motives

7. Without apology if given in good faith.

In receiving constructive criticism you should:

1. remain quiet and listen

2. not find fault with the criticising person

3. not manipulate the appraiser by your response (eg despair)

4. not try to change the subject

5. not caricature the complaint

6. not ascribe an ulterior motive to the appraiser

7. give the impression you understand the point.

In handling criticism you should accept it and not ignore, deny or deflect it.

Managing meetings

Meetings are much maligned, but are they usually approached and handled as they should be?

In general terms any meeting needs:

- planning
- informality
- participation
- purpose
- leadership

if it is to work, and that is so whether the meeting is in committee or conference format.

A meeting must have a purpose and this can be one (or all) of the following:

- to pool available information
- to make decisions
- to let off steam/tension
- to change attitudes
- to instruct/teach.

Meetings must be prepared for:

1. Know in advance what information, reports, agenda, lay-out, technical data or equipment is required

2. Be clear about the purpose

3. Inform other participants of the purpose and share, in advance, relevant information/ documents

4. Have a timetable and agenda (and notify others in advance)

5. Identify main topics with each having an objective

6. Make necessary housekeeping arrangements.

Chairing a meeting means that you should guide and control it having defined the purpose of it, gatekeeping the discussions as appropriate (opening it to some, closing it when necessary), summarising, interpreting and concluding it with agreed decisions, on time.

The chairman's role in leading/refereeing effective meetings is to ensure that the following elements are handled correctly:

1. ***Aim*** – after starting on time, to outline purpose clearly

2. ***Plan*** – to prepare the agenda (and allocate time)

3. ***Guide*** – to ensure effective discussion

4. ***Crystallize*** – to establish conclusions

5. ***Act*** – to gain acceptance and commitment and then to end on time.

Meetings are groupings of people and can develop their own personality. It can help to understand the personality of a particular grouping by reference to group:

• conformity

• values

• attitude to change

- prejudice
- power.

So that the method of running the meeting and its effectiveness depends on understanding and overcoming the problems posed by the group personality.

Within your organisation

Organisations have a degree of permanence, hierarchy and formal communication. Informal communication supplements the formal communication that is needed in organisations.

The **content** of communication in organisations should be (in relation to):

1. The task
- the purpose, aims and objectives
- plans
- progress and prospects

2. The team
- changes in structure and deployment
- ways to improve team work
- ethos and values

3. The individual
- pay and conditions
- safety, health and welfare
- education and training

The **direction** of flows of communication within an organisation must be downward, upward and sideways.

Decisions on what to communicate should bear in mind the must-know priorities and distinguish them from the should-know or could-know lower priorities. The best method for must-know items is face-to-face backed by the written word.

Two-way communication should be used and encouraged to:

* Communicate plans/changes/progress/ prospects

* Give employees the opportunity to change/ improve management decisions (before they are made)

* Use the experience and ideas of employees to the full

* Understand the other side's point of view.

Summary and six-month follow-up test

Summary

i)   Personal reminders

Effective speaking – six key principles:

1.   Be clear

2.   Be prepared

3.   Be simple

4.   Be vivid

5.   Be natural

6.   Be concise

Practical presentation skills require you to:

• profile the occasion, audience and location

• plan and write the presentation

• use visual aids (if appropriate)

• prepare your talk

• rehearse (with others if necessary)

• deliver on the day.

Good communicators are skilled at listening by:

• being willing to listen

• hearing the message

• interpreting the meaning

• evaluating carefully

• responding appropriately.

Effective writing has three elements:

1. Structure
2. Layout
3. Style.

and also needs the six key principles of:

1. Clarity
2. Planning
3. Preparation
4. Simplicity
5. Vividness
6. Naturalness
7. Conciseness.

Six month follow-up test

Can you calmly plan for meetings?

Has your performance as a communicator improved and do you listen more?

Have you identified and addressed communication/ presentation strengths/weaknesses of yourself and key members of your team?

Have meetings (one-to-one and others) improved?

Has written communication improved in your organisation?

5 Personal reminders and thoughts worth thinking

Introduction

This section will look at the main areas covered in this pocketbook and will offer:

i) personal reminders – points to bear in mind in pursuing your personal development as a leader, motivator and communicator; and

ii) thoughts worth thinking – quotes from various sources which shed light on management and leadership topics covered, which you might find helpful or inspiring.

Leadership

Personal reminders

Whether in team, operational or organisational leadership, what matters is:

- The leader – qualities of personality and character

- The situation – partly constant, partly varying

- The team – the followers: their needs and values

Three overlapping and interacting circles of needs
have to be focused on at all times:

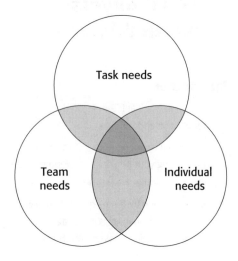

Leadership functions (and the skills needed to exercise those skills) can be summarised as:

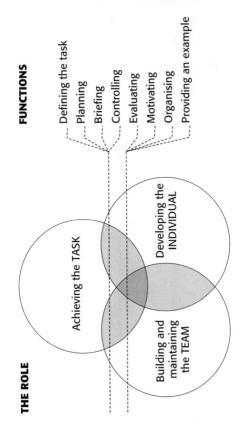

FUNCTIONS

Defining the task
Planning
Briefing
Controlling
Evaluating
Motivating
Organising
Providing an example

THE ROLE

Achieving the TASK

Developing the INDIVIDUAL

Building and maintaining the TEAM

Teambuilding

Personal reminders

Leaders should consider these issues in teambuilding:

Achieving the task

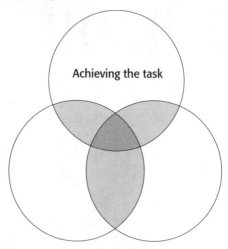

- Purpose
- Responsibilities
- Objectives
- Programme
- Working conditions
- Resources
- Targets
- Authority

- Training
- Priorities
- Progress
- Supervision
- Setting an example.

Building and maintaining the team

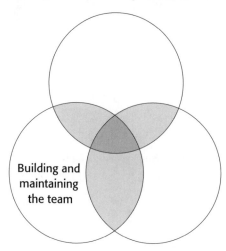

Building and
maintaining
the team

- Objectives
- Standards
- Safety standards
- Size of team
- Team members
- Team spirit
- Discipline

- Grievances
- Consultation
- Briefing
- Representing
- Supporting.

Developing the individual

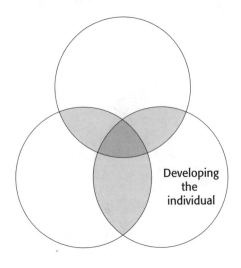

- Targets
- Induction
- Achievement
- Responsibilities
- Authority
- Training
- Recognition
- Growth
- Performance
- Reward
- The task
- The person

- Time/attention
- Grievances
- Security
- Appraisal.

Leadership

Thoughts worth thinking

'Courage is the quality
that guarantees
all others.'

Churchill

'Leadership is done
from in front.' Peter Young

'*As* to moral courage, I have rarely met with the two-
o'-clock-in-the-morning kind: I mean unprepared
courage, that which is necessary on an unexpected
occasion; and which, in spite of the most unforeseen
events, leaves full freedom of judgement and decision.'

Napoleon

'President Roosevelt possessed personality, but as his nation's leader... he also did his homework – thoroughly.'

'A sense of humility is a quality I have observed in every leader I have deeply admired.'

Dwight D Eisenhower

'Is there not a difference between good leaders and leaders for good?'

John Lord

Making Time to Think

'What advice can be offered to a leader? He must discipline himself and lead a carefully regulated and ordered life. He must allow a certain amount of time for quiet thought and reflection; the best times are in the early morning, and in the evening. The quality, good or bad, of any action which is to be taken will vary directly with the time spent in thinking; against this, he must not be rigid; his decisions and plans must be adaptable to changing situations. A certain ruthlessness is essential, particularly with inefficiency and also with those who would waste his time. People will accept this, provided the leader is ruthless with himself...

Most leaders will find there is so much to do and so little time to do it; that was my experience in the military sphere. My answer to that is not to worry; what is needed is a quiet contemplation of all aspects of the problem, followed by a decision — and it is fatal to worry afterwards.'

Field Marshal Viscount Montgomery

'A leader is best

When people barely know that he exists.

Not so good when people obey and acclaim him

Worst when they despise him

'Fail to honour people, they fail to honour you,'

But of a good leader, who talks little,

When his work is done, his aim fulfilled,

They will all say, 'we did this ourselves.'

Lao Tzu • 6th century BC

'Leaders should not be easily provoked.' St Paul

'Quiet calm deliberation disentangles every knot.'

Harold MacMillan

'The test of leadership is not to put greatness into humanity but to elicit it, for the greatness is there already.'

John Buchan

'He that gives good advice builds with one hand. He that gives good counsel and example builds with both. But he that gives good admonition and bad example, builds with one hand and pulls down with the other.'

Francis Bacon

'It is almost true to say that leaders are 'made' – rather than born.'

Field Marshal Viscount Montgomery

'In managing human affairs, there is no better rule than self-restraint.'

Lao Tzu • 6th Century BC

'A good leader must be tough enough to win a fight, but not tough enough to kick a man when he is down.' W G Bennis and E H Schein

'A good leader must be tough enough to win a fight, but not tough enough to kick a man when he is down.' W G Bennis and E H Schein • 'A good leader must be tough enough to win a fight, but not tough enough to kick a man when he is down.' W G Bennis and E H Schein • 'A good leader must be tough enough to win a fight, but not tough enough to kick a man when he is down.' W G Bennis and E H Schein • 'A good leader must be tough enough to win a fight, but not tough enough to kick a man when he is down.' W G Bennis and E H Schein • 'A good leader must be tough enough to win a fight, but not tough enough to kick a man when he is down.' W G Bennis and E H

THE PRAYER OF A FAMOUS LEADER

'Lord, make me an instrument of your peace!

Where there is hatred, let me sow love,

Where there is injury, pardon;

Where there is doubt, faith;

Where there is despair, hope;

Where there is darkness, light;

Where there is sadness, joy.

O Divine Master, grant that I may not so much seek

to be consoled, as to console;

to be understood, as to understand;

to be loved, as to love.

For it is in giving that we receive;

It is in pardoning that we are pardoned;

It is in dying that we are born to eternal life.'

Francis of Assisi

'If you can keep your head when those about you are losing theirs and blaming it on

you.'

Kipling

'Your position never gives you the right to command. It only imposes on you the duty of so living your life that others can receive your orders without being humiliated.'

Dag Hammarskjold

Teambuilding

Thoughts worth thinking

'You do not know me, I do not know you, but we have got to work together. Therefore, we must understand each other, we must have confidence in each other. I have only been here a few hours, but from what I have seen and heard since I arrived, I am prepared to say here and now that I have confidence in you. We will work together as a team. I believe that one of the first duties is to create what I call atmosphere. I do not like the general atmosphere I find here – it is an atmosphere of doubt, of looking back. All that must cease. I want to impress upon everyone that the bad times are over and it will be done. If anybody here thinks it cannot be done, let him go at once. I do not want any doubters. It can be done and it will be done beyond any possibility of doubt.'

Field Marshal Viscount Montgomery

Extract from speech to staff in taking over the Eighth Army, before the Battle of El Alamein

MORALE

Morale
>Shows itself
>As a state of mind
>Radiating confidence
>In people

Where each member
>Feels sure of his own niche,
>Stands on his own abilities
>And works out his own solutions
>– Knowing he is
>Part of a team

Where no person
>Feels anxiety or fear
>Or pressure to be better
>Than someone else

Where there exists
>A sharing of ideas
>A freedom to plan
>A sureness of worth,
>And a knowledge
>That help is available
>For the asking

To the end that
>People grow and mature
>Warmed by a friendly climate

Anon

'Light is the task, when many share the toil.'

Homer

Motivation and people management

Personal reminders

To draw the best out of people the key strategies are:

- Be motivated yourself
- Select people who are already motivated
- Set challenging but realistic targets
- Remember that progress motivates
- Treat each person as an individual
- Provide fair rewards
- Give recognition

Thoughts worth thinking

'The two great movers
of the human mind are
the desire of good and
the fear of evil.'

Samuel Johnson

'I am persuaded that every being

has a part to play on earth:

to be exact, his or her own part

which resembles no other.'

André Gide

'Such is the state of life

that none are happy but by

the anticipation of change.'

Samuel Johnson

'A man has one eye on what he gives, but seven eyes on what he receives.'

Old German Proverb

'A man's **reach** should **exceed** his **grasp.**'

Robert Browning

'If you treat people as they are, they will stay as they are. But if you treat them as they ought to be, they will become bigger and better persons.'

Goethe

'Give me a **fire** and **I will give you light**.'

Old Arab Proverb

'**Nothing great was ever achieved without enthusiasm.**'

Emerson

'No man will find the best way to do a thing unless he loves to do that thing.'

Old Japanese Proverb

'It is not enough to do our best.

Sometimes we have to do what is required.'

Churchill

'Management, above everything else,
is about people. It is about the
accomplishment of ends and aims by
the efforts of groups of people working
together. The people and their individual
hopes and skills are the greatest variable
and the most important one.'

Sir John Harvey-Jones

'You get more of the behaviour you

reward. You don't get what you hope

for, ask for, wish for, or beg for. You

get what you reward.'

Michel le Boeuf

'Fame is the spur that the clear spirit doth raise...

To scorn delights and live laborious days.'

Milton

'Any of us

will put out more

and better ideas

if our efforts

are fully appreciated.'

Alexander F Osborn

'No man does anything from a single motive.'

Samuel Taylor Coleridge

'BY ASKING THE
IMPOSSIBLE

WE OBTAIN
THE BEST POSSIBLE.'

Italian proverb

'All

that we do

is done

with an eye

to something else.'

Aristotle

The leader as decision-maker

i) Personal reminders

- The ability to take decisions – the most valuable skill in management

- The five point plan:

    - Define objective

    - Check information

    - Develop options

    - Evaluate and decide

    - Implement.

- Use: analysis, holistic thinking, thinking in concepts, imagination, valuing (truth), intuition, your unconscious mind, options, argument, originality

- Know your mind and develop your thinking skills.

ii) Thoughts worth thinking

'If I have any advice to pass on it is this: if one wants to be successful one must think until it hurts... Believe me, this is hard work and, from my close observation, I can say that there are few people indeed who are prepared to perform this arduous and tiring work.'　　Roy Thomson

'When I go into any business deal my chief thoughts are on how I'm going to save myself if things go wrong.'

Paul Getty

‘The **final** act of **business** judgement is **intuitive.**’

Anon

'I take it we are all in complete agreement on the decision here ... then, I propose we postpone further discussion of this matter until our next meeting to give ourselves time to develop disagreement and perhaps gain some understanding of what the decision is about!' Alfred P Sloan

'Rightly to be great
is not to stir without
great argument.'

Shakespeare

'Men sleep well in the Inn of Decision.'

Old Arab Proverb

Communication and presentation

Personal reminders

Effective speaking – six key principles:

1. Be clear
2. Be prepared
3. Be simple
4. Be vivid
5. Be natural
6. Be concise

Practical presentation skills require you to:

- profile the occasion, audience and location
- plan and write the presentation
- use visual aids (if appropriate)
- prepare your talk
- rehearse (with others if necessary)
- deliver on the day

Good communicators are skilled at listening by:

- being willing to listen
- hearing the message
- interpreting the meaning
- evaluating carefully
- responding appropriately

Effective writing has three elements:

1. Structure
2. Layout
3. Style

and also needs the six key principles of:

1. Clarity
2. Planning
3. Preparation
4. Simplicity
5. Vividness
6. Naturalness
7. Conciseness.

Thoughts worth thinking

'Speak properly,

and in as few words

as you can,

but always plainly;

for the end of speech is not

ostentation,

but to be understood.'

William Penn

'Communication is the art of being **UNDERSTOOD**.'

Peter Ustinov

'What is conceived well is
expressed clearly

And words to say it
will arise with ease.'

Nicholas Boileau

'If any man wishes to write in a
clear style, let him first be clear
in his thoughts.' Goethe

'Have something to say

and say it as clearly as you can.

That is the only secret of style.'

Matthew Arnold

'Reading is to the **mind**

what **exercise** is to the **body.'**

English Proverb

'The major mistake in

communication

is to believe that it

happens'

George Bernard Shaw

'In good communication, people should be in no doubt that you have reached a **conclusion**.'

John Adair and Neil Thomas

Hawksmere Publishing

Hawksmere publishes a wide range of books, reports, special briefings, psychometric tests and videos. Listed below is a selection of key titles.

Masters in Management

Mastering business planning and strategy
Paul Elkin £19.99

Mastering financial management
Stephen Brookson £19.99

Mastering leadership
Michael Williams £19.99

Mastering negotiations
Eric Evans £19.99

Mastering people management
Mark Thomas £19.99

Mastering project management
Cathy Lake £19.99

Mastering Personal and Interpersonal Skills
Peter Haddon £16.99

Mastering Marketing
Ian Ruskin-Brown £19.99

Other titles

The inside track to successful management
Dr Gerald Kushel £16.95

The pension trustee's handbook (2nd edition)
Robin Ellison £25

Sales management and organisation
Peter Green £9.99

Time management and personal development
John Adair and Melanie Allen £9.99

Everything you need for an NVQ in
management – *Julie Lewthwaite* £19.99

The management tool kit
Sultan Kermally £10.99

Working smarter
Graham Roberts-Phelps £15.99

Desktop Guides

The company director's desktop guide
David Martin £15.99

The company secretary's desktop guide
Roger Mason £15.99

The credit controller's desktop guide
Roger Mason £15.99

The finance and accountancy desktop guide
Ralph Tiffin £15.99

Reports and Special Briefings

Dynamic budgetary control
David Allen £95

Evaluating and monitoring strategies
David Allen £95

Software licence agreements
Robert Bond £125

Negotiation tactics for software and
hi-tech agreements
Robert Bond £165

Achieving business excellence, quality and
performance improvement
Colin Chapman and Dennis Hopper £95

Compliance with CDM regulations
Stuart Macdougald-Denton £125

Employment law aspects of mergers
and acquisitions – *Michael Ryley* £125

Mergers and acquisitions – confronting
the organisation and people issues
Mark Thomas £125

An employer's guide to the management of
complaints of sex and race discrimination
Christopher Walter £125

Securing business funding from
Europe and the UK
Peter Wilding £125

Influencing the European Union
Peter Wilding £125

Standard conditions of commercial contract
Peter Wilding £139

To order any title, or to request more information,
please call Hawksmere Customer Services on 0207
824 8257 or fax on 0207 730 4293.